Rev It Up!

HOT RODS

by **Thomas K. Adamson**

Consulting Editor: Gail Saunders-Smith, PhD

Consultant: Leslie Kendall, Curator
Petersen Automotive Museum, Los Angeles

CAPSTONE PRESS
a capstone imprint

Pebble Plus is published by Capstone Press,
151 Good Counsel Drive, P.O. Box 669, Mankato, Minnesota 56002.
www.capstonepub.com

Books published by Capstone Press are manufactured with paper
containing at least 10 percent post-consumer waste.

Library of Congress Cataloging-in-Publication Data
Adamson, Thomas K., 1970–
   Hot rods / by Thomas K. Adamson.
      p. cm.—(Pebble plus. Rev it up!)
   Includes bibliographical references and index.
   Summary: "Simple text and full-color photographs briefly describe the history and unique features of hot rods"—
Provided by publisher.
   ISBN 978-1-4296-5317-6 (library binding)
   1. Hot rods—Juvenile literature. I. Title. II. Series.
   TL236.3.A24 2011
   629.228'6—dc22

                                                        2010025023

Editorial Credits

Erika L. Shores, editor; Ted Williams, designer; Laura Manthe, production specialist

Photo Credits

Alamy/Cynthia Lindow, 7; Performance Image, 17
BigStockPhoto.com/digitalphotoart, 15
Corbis/Seattle Post-Intelligencer Collection/Museum of History and Industry, 9
Getty Images Inc./Time & Life Pictures/Ralph Crane, 11
KimballStock/Ron Kimball, cover, 19, 21
Shutterstock/glen gaffney, 13; Jonathan Timar, 1; Shotgun, 5

Artistic Effects

Shutterstock/Alexander Chaikin, argus, cajoer, Robert Elias

Note to Parents and Teachers

The Rev It Up! series supports national social studies standards related to science, technology,
and society. This book describes and illustrates hot rods. The images support early readers
in understanding the text. The repetition of words and phrases helps early readers learn new
words. This book also introduces early readers to subject-specific vocabulary words, which are
defined in the Glossary section. Early readers may need assistance to read some words and to
use the Table of Contents, Glossary, Read More, Internet Sites, and Index sections of the book.

Printed in the United States of America in North Mankato, Minnesota.

092010   005933CGS11

Table of Contents

Stylish Rides

A hot rod is an old car that has been fixed up to go fast. Almost any old car or truck can be made into a hot rod.

Hot rodders add their own style to their cars. A new or tuned-up engine makes it faster. A fancy paint job makes it look cooler.

Hot Rod History

Hot rods were once built

by people who couldn't afford

a new car. They found

an old car and did

their own work on it.

People with these fixed-up cars
started using them for
drag races. From a standstill,
two hot rods sped down
a straight road or track.

Parts of a Hot Rod

Some hot rod owners chop
the top off their cars.
Short windows make the car
look low and sleek.

13

Owners often put in a large engine. Taking off the hood lets everyone see and hear the engine. Rumble! Rumble!

A hot rod's paint job is
a work of art.

Hot rods often have flames
painted on the sides.

For most people, a hot rod

is all about shine.

Exhaust pipes and wheel rims

made of shiny chrome

grab people's attention.

Rev It Up!

Hot rodders love the look

of an old car made

to be flashy and fast!

Vroom! Vroom!

Glossary

chrome—a coating that gives car parts a shiny, metallic look

drag race—a race in which two cars begin at a standstill and drive in a straight line at high speeds for a short distance

engine—a machine in which fuel burns to provide power to move something

exhaust pipe—a part of a car where the waste gases made by the engine come out

hood—the part of the car that opens and closes and usually covers the engine

rim—the metal part of a wheel on which the tire goes

style—the way in which something is done

Read More

Braun, Eric. *Hot Rods*. Motor Mania. Minneapolis: Lerner Publications Co., 2007.

Poolos, J. *Wild about Hot Rods*. Wild Rides. New York: PowerKids Press, 2008.

Internet Sites

FactHound offers a safe, fun way to find Internet sites related to this book. All of the sites on FactHound have been researched by our staff.

Here's all you do:

Visit *www.facthound.com*

Type in this code: 9781429653176

Super-cool stuff!
Check out projects, games and lots more at
www.capstonekids.com

Index

Word Count: 201

Grade: 1

Early-Intervention Level: 17